THE WESTERN WAY

Western Steam in the Sixties

Photographs and text by
Terence Dorrity

Irwell Press Ltd.

THE WESTERN WAY

Western Steam in the Sixties — Photographs by Terence Dorrity

I had been fascinated by steam locomotives from an early age. This probably had its origin when my mother took me to our local station at Henley-in-Arden to see the Royal Train go past on what was, I believe, the visit by King George VI, Queen Elizabeth and Princess Margaret to Stratford-upon-Avon on the 20 April 1950. I have since learned, thanks to the Shakespeare Centre archive service, that the train was headed by two ex GWR Castles, 5000 *Launceston Castle* and 5035 *Coity Castle.* The members of the Royal Family were not even on board at the time as the train was on its way to Tyseley for servicing but as I was just under four years old it was the royal engines that impressed me. Later we moved to Stratford-upon-Avon and around this time my paternal grandfather worked for the Tothill Press in London. He was in the advertising department which presumably dealt with all their titles but one of them was the *Railway Magazine* and he would give me a copy when I saw him. The points were set for an enduring interest.

At Stratford-upon-Avon I discovered a band of fellow 'train-spotters'. The strange hobby of noting down locomotive numbers was, at that time, at least as popular a hobby as stamp collecting or following a football team. This enthusiasm was reinforced by a thriving King Edward VI School railway society which, among other activities, organised visits to Swindon Works. Tantalising glimpses of what could be seen elsewhere in the country were provided by a very popular BBC TV series called *Railway Roundabout*. A great treat was a very occasional journey up to London with my mother and my dog-eared Ian Allan Western Region Locospotters' book. This meant catching a local train to Leamington Spa to change to a Birmingham Snow Hill to Paddington express. Well dressed for a trip to town with, of course, a hat, as was the habit of the day, she was really there for the shops but we never failed to go up to the driver on the footplate of his King to say 'thank you'. Many people did and some businessmen would even give him a tip. Stratford was well placed for the youthful Great Western enthusiast as it was on the ex GWR line from the Midlands to South Wales and the West Country and it was just a short train or bicycle ride away from the Paddington to Birmingham Snow Hill and Wolverhampton Low Level main line with its Kings and Castles storming Hatton Bank. On Friday 6 May 1960, Princess Margaret married Antony Armstrong-Jones at Westminster Abbey. It was the first royal wedding to be broadcast on television but as we were given the day off school the Kings at Hatton were the royalty that interested us the most. I clearly remember our location on the footbridge over the main line at the North Junction. Someone had a relatively early transistor radio and *Get Me to the Church on Time* from *My Fair Lady,* which although not yet a film was a big hit in the West End and on Broadway, was being played over and over again along with the Everly Brothers' *Cathy's Clown* and Lonnie Donegan's recently released *My Old Man's a Dustman* on Housewives' Choice etc on the BBC Light Programme. There were, of course, visits to engine sheds. Sometimes this involved the time-honoured 'bunking' but usually, for the bigger sheds at least, we were armed with the flimsy, airmail paper type, permits which were fairly generously provided if requested for in advance. Sometimes we found simply asking the shed foreman was enough to gain entry, though this was definitely not always the case. I was fortunate in that my parents indulged my hobby from time to time. I recall an occasion when I was in

7003 ELMLEY CASTLE waits for duty on its home shed, Gloucester Horton Road (85B), during April 1963.

Bristol with my mother for some reason I cannot now remember but I badgered her to let me visit Bath Road engine shed. I must have been about twelve and the foreman arranged for someone to show me round but told my mother that it was considered to be bad luck for women to be in the shed. Whether or not this was a joke, she sat in the mess nursing a mug of engineman's tea while I noted down the numbers of the sixty or so locomotives present. It was her one and only shed visit! On another occasion my father drove me and some friends to Aberystwyth visiting various sheds on the way even though he was not in the least interested himself.

The 'flagship' service calling at Stratford-upon-Avon was the weekdays only Cornishman, one of British Railways' named trains of the period. In the northbound direction it ran all the way from Penzance via Plymouth, Exeter, Bristol, Gloucester Eastgate and Cheltenham Spa Malvern Road and on to Birmingham Snow Hill before ending its long journey at Wolverhampton Low Level. It was scheduled to leave Stratford just after six in the evening and it attracted quite a number of us to the station on weekdays to see the Castle in charge. There was, of course, a Cornishman in the opposite direction but since it left Stratford at twenty past ten in the morning, in term time at least, its devotees could only listen out for the familiar whistle while sitting at their school desks. The Cornishman had been introduced on this route in 1952 but much changed with the start of the Winter timetable in 1962. From 10 September its northern starting point was moved from Wolverhampton Low Level to Sheffield and it was diverted via Birmingham New Street and along the ex Midland Railway line through Bromsgrove and so no longer served Stratford. On the last day that the Cornishman ran through the town, on Friday 7 September 1962, Castle class 7001 *Sir James Milne*, with Grange class 6861 *Crynant Grange* piloting out of Stratford, had the honour of hauling the train and there is a photograph recording the moment in this book.

On Summer Saturdays, as well as unnamed trains serving the Cornishman destinations, you could travel direct to Paignton, Weston-super-Mare, Ilfracombe and Minehead. Loads could be heavy and double-heading or banking was not uncommon in the Birmingham direction because of the gradient to Wilmcote. There were also trains from Birmingham Snow Hill which ran via Cheltenham Malvern Road and Gloucester Central to Cardiff General, Swansea High Street and Carmarthen, with through carriages all the way to Pembroke Dock on some services. Until the late 1950s a number of South Wales services were operated with ex-GWR wartime built two-car streamlined buffet and toilet equipped diesel railcars with an added carriage between them while others were steam hauled. Unfortunately, like the Cornishman, this service was diverted away from Stratford in September 1962 but this was not before I and other local railway enthusiasts had taken advantage of it. During the 1959 Summer school holiday a friend and I managed to get the ticket of our dreams, a Western Region Rail Rover, and although, at 13, our mothers insisted we return home every evening we were well placed to cover a large part of the region, much of it behind steam. Gloucester was also a favourite destination with its mix of ex GWR and LMSR services and the associated Horton Road and Barnwood sheds. A little later, when an older member of our group who had obtained his driving licence hired a car for the day on a couple of occasions, we set off in the black Austin A40 Farina via the exciting and almost deserted new Ross Spur M50 motorway to visit the BR engine sheds and National Coal Board colliery railway systems in the South Wales valleys.

In addition to the long distance cross-country trains through Stratford there were local ones to Worcester via Evesham and, as is still the case today, trains to Leamington Spa via Hatton and to Birmingham Moor Street and Snow Hill stations along the North Warwickshire line via Henley-in-Arden. Sadly for steam enthusiasts, except for a few notable exceptions, diesel multiple units such as class 116 DMUs and class 121 'bubble cars' were employed on these services by the early sixties. Some venerable ex GWR railcars had earlier worked on Worcester locals before replacement by more modern BR types. There remained quite a lot of railway action through the town, however, with a wide variety of interesting steam motive power to be seen on regular heavy iron ore and other freight trains, Summer Saturday West of England services on one of the last routes to see regular Castle workings, on banking duties and on excursion trains from all over the country for the 1964 Shakespeare anniversary celebrations. A small number of local passenger trains also stayed firmly in the hands of steam for a few more years.

Stratford was something of a railway crossroads at the time because there was another line running from east to west. This was the old Stratford-upon-Avon and Midland Junction Railway (SMJR), which became part of the London Midland and Scottish Railway (LMSR) at the grouping

Prairie 4100, passes Horton Road shed in Gloucester on a Cheltenham bound train on Saturday 1 February 1964.

in 1923. The railway station, Stratford Old Town, had seen its last regular passenger train in 1952 but its paintwork was refreshed and potholes in the platform filled in for the arrival of the Queen Mother on 11 July 1964 when she visited the town for the official opening of the restored Stratford Canal. A few enthusiasts' specials also stopped there before the closure of the line. The route had been kept open for freight workings which crossed over the main line on a bridge and continued through to Broom Junction on the Birmingham to Evesham line until a 'new' curve between the Old Town station and the main line was opened in 1960 to shorten the distance for trains carrying iron ore to South Wales. Granges, Halls and ex-GWR 2-8-0s worked these along with WD 2-8-0s, Standard 9Fs and ex LMS 8Fs. Despite this investment, the SMJR line was closed in 1965.

7919 RUNTER HALL has clearly just been outshopped at Swindon Works on Sunday 7 April 1963.

The realisation that the railway scene was about to change forever with the introduction of more diesel locomotives and multiple units, later reinforced by the publication of the Beeching Report 'The Reshaping of British Railways' on 27 March 1963, had prompted a number of erstwhile 'train-spotters' who had become more serious railway enthusiasts to join the few old hands who were already doing so and record on film the last days of what was then still the common sight of steam and, like them, in my teens and early twenties I followed up my initial interest and did the same. As you will see from the photographs in this book, I had the chance to photograph a range of ex GWR types over much of the Western Region and the parts of it which were transferred to the London Midland Region in 1963. Even after the end of steam on BR there was still the opportunity to witness 1500 and 5700 class examples working in National Coal Board ownership and more 5700 pannier tanks on the London Underground until the early years of the next decade. The record holder was ex GWR pannier tank 7754 which was not withdrawn until 1975. I was sent to Mountain Ash Comprehensive School as a trainee teacher in 1971 when 7754 was still very much in action working alongside saddle tanks at the local colliery and visible through the classroom window. Bliss!

I had taken earlier black and white photographs with my trusty Kodak Brownie 127 roll film camera before I graduated to 35mm when I obtained a Kodak Retinette. Limited colour slide film followed in 1960 when the rather slow, but I now realise colour stable over time, 12 ASA Kodachrome was the most popular brand. This was replaced by Kodachrome II and Kodachrome X with, each time, an increase in ASA speed which was obviously useful when photographing moving trains. I tried other makes in small quantities, Ilford, Perutz, High Speed Ektachrome, but relied mainly on Kodachrome and Agfa CT18. Earlier photos taken on Agfa film have lasted the fifty years or so reasonably well but some of the later ones have very annoyingly suffered badly from colour deterioration and can be grainy so have not been suitable for this book. I used the three different cameras shown in the picture over the period covered, the final one being the SLR.

Terence Dorrity, 2020

(left) Taron Marquise 35mm camera: Taronar 1:1.8 45mm lens
(centre) Kodak Retinette 35mm camera: Schneider-Kreuznach Reomar 1:3.5 45mm lens
(right) Mamiya, Prismat CPH, 35mm SLR camera: Mamiya Sekor 1:1.9 48mm lens

5206 is shunting in the massive marshalling yard at Pontypool Road on Monday 12 April 1965.

CONTENTS

Part One: Ex Great Western Railway Tender Engines

1. 4-6-0s on Express Passenger Trains.. 6

2. Local Passenger Services... 26

3. Delivering the Goods... 39

4. On Shed and at the Works.. 55

5. Excursion Trains and Enthusiast Specials... 66

Part Two: Ex Great Western Railway Tank Engines

6. Ex-GWR Saddle Tanks.. 79

Including those originally belonging to dock and harbour railways absorbed into the GWR.

7. 5700 type 0-6-0 Pannier Tank:.. 85

In BR, London Transport and National Coal Board service.

8. Other types of ex-GWR Pannier Tank:.. 97

Including some survivors in industrial use.

9. Side Tanks:... 108

Various types of ex-GWR 'Prairie', 0-6-2, 2-8-0 and 0-4-2 tank locomotive.

Fortunately, I kept detailed notes at the time I took the photographs and I found the following useful for additional information:
- The relevant British Railways Western and London Midland Region timetables.
- The Great Western Archive: http://www.greatwestern.org.uk/index.htm
- BR steam locomotive index: http://www.brdatabase.info
- Rail UK: http://www.railuk.info
- Six Bells Junction: The Railtour Files: http://www.sixbellsjunction.co.uk
- *Indian Summer of Wolverhampton (Oxley) Castles.* Steve Bartlett. *Steam Days* April 2015
- Warwickshire Railways: http://www.warwickshirerailways.com
- Industrial Railway Society books: *Industrial Locomotives of West Glamorgan*, *Industrial Locomotives of Mid and South Glamorgan* and *Industrial Locomotives of Gwent*.
- and the websites of the preserved lines mentioned.

Shed codes shown are those that applied on the date the photographs were taken. Many ex GW sheds in the Midlands were recoded as LMR depots and some Southern ones were transferred to the Western Region in September 1963.

Copyright IRWELL PRESS LIMITED
ISBN-978-1-911262-37-4
First published in the United Kingdom in 2020
by Irwell Press Limited, 59A, High Street, Clophill,
Bedfordshire MK45 4BE
Printed by Akcent Media, UK
Tel: 01525 861888
www.irwellpress.com

Ex-Great Western Railway Tender Engines
1: 4-6-0s on Express Passenger Trains

7001 SIR JAMES MILNE is piloted by 6861 CRYNANT GRANGE past the East signal box and the gas holder at Stratford-upon-Avon on Friday 7 September 1962. This was the last *Cornishman* from Penzance to Wolverhampton Low Level to run through the town because after this date this train was diverted onto the Midland line from Cheltenham to Birmingham New Street. Castle class 7001 entered service in 1945 as DENBIGH CASTLE but it was renamed after the General Manager of the GWR early in 1948. It was withdrawn in September 1963. Tyseley (84E) allocated Collett designed Grange 6861, which entered service in 1939 and was withdrawn in October 1965, had been attached at Stratford to assist with the 1 in 75 climb up Wilmcote Bank.

5026 CRICCIETH CASTLE approaches Stratford-upon-Avon station in the Summer of 1962. The chalked headcode 1H25 indicates it was hauling the Saturdays only 14:08 departure from Weston-super-Mare Locking Road station to Wolverhampton Low Level where it was due to arrive at 18:17. It left Stratford at 16:54. Wolverhampton Stafford Road (84A) shedded 5026 entered service in 1934 and it was withdrawn in November 1964 and scrapped at Cashmore's of Great Bridge.

Looking in need of a good clean, Wolverhampton Stafford Road (84A) shedded 7024 POWIS CASTLE was at Stratford-upon-Avon at 19:00 on 10 August 1963. This was just two days after the notorious 'Great Train Robbery'. Train 1H34 was the Summer Saturdays only 11:20 Newquay to Wolverhampton Low Level where it was due to arrive at 19:56 but it was running twenty-five minutes late. POWIS CASTLE was built in 1949 and withdrawn in February 1965 and cut up at Cashmore's of Great Bridge.

7011 BANBURY CASTLE had been transferred from Worcester (85A) to Oxley (2B) depot to reinforce the Castle fleet the month before this photograph was taken. Seen at Wilmcote on train 1V53, the Summer Saturdays only 08:00 Wolverhampton Low Level to Ilfracombe, on 4 July 1964, it was due to leave Stratford-upon-Avon at 09:21 and arrive in Ilfracombe at 15:35. This was the last Summer for the Castle locomotives on the West of England expresses. 7011 was built in 1948, withdrawn in February 1965 and scrapped by Cashmore's at Great Bridge.

7019 FOWEY CASTLE on the Saturdays only train 1V52 coasts along near Stratford-upon-Avon at Bishopton, at the end of the descent of the 1 in 75 Wilmcote Bank, on 20 June 1964. The train had left Wolverhampton Low Level on its nine hour fifty-five minute journey at 06:55 and it was due to arrive in Penzance at 16:50. 7019 was built in 1949 and, like BANBURY CASTLE, it was allocated to Oxley shed (2B), withdrawn in February 1965 and cut up by Cashmore's at Great Bridge.

Wolverhampton Stafford Road (84A) allocated Castle class 5089 WESTMINSTER ABBEY runs down Hatton Bank on the 'Pines Express' on Saturday 27 April 1963. This train left Manchester Piccadilly at 10:00 and ran via Birmingham Snow Hill, Reading West and Southampton Central to Bournemouth West where it was due to arrive at 17:18. Until the previous year the 'Pines' had run over the Somerset and Dorset line. The locomotive was built as Star class 4069 in 1923 but was rebuilt as a Castle in 1939. It was withdrawn in November 1964 and scrapped at Cashmore's at Great Bridge.

7029 CLUN CASTLE approaches Kings Sutton Junction on Friday 11 June 1965 in charge of the very last regular steam passenger train out of Paddington. This was train M48, the Monday to Friday only 16:15 from Paddington which was due to arrive at Banbury at 18:40-and it was the last day of this service before the introduction of the Summer timetable. The line joining on the right is the Banbury and Cheltenham Direct Railway, most of which had already closed but a short section remained open until 1969 as a main line connection for ironstone trains from Adderbury.

CLUN CASTLE again on the rather sad but historic last regular steam passenger train from Paddington at Kings Sutton on Friday 11 June 1965. Kings Sutton Junction signal box can be seen just before the overbridge which carries a farm track. Built by British Railways in 1950, 7029 was the last of the class to be withdrawn, in December 1965. It was bought for preservation and is now based at the Tyseley Locomotive Works in Birmingham.

Worcester (85A) allocated 7027 THORNBURY CASTLE pulls away from Paddington under the old Bishop's Bridge which was lifted in 2004 and replaced by a wider structure in 2005. This train, on Sunday 7 July 1963, was probably bound for Worcester. 7027 was built by British Railways in 1949 and withdrawn a little over fourteen years later, in December 1963. It was sold for scrap to Woodham Bros of Barry where it joined the sad lines of locomotives awaiting disposal. However, like most of the others which have since been reprieved, THORNBURY CASTLE left Barry in August 1972. It has still not been restored although work is now underway to return it to traffic and it is likely to be based on the Great Central Railway.

Hall class 4-6-0 5958 KNOLTON HALL has just passed under the Paddington to Worcester main line at Honeybourne heading towards Cheltenham on a passenger train in 1961. This section of line, closed in 1976, may one day be reopened as an extension of the Gloucestershire Warwickshire Railway. 5958 was shedded at Old Oak Common (81A) at the time. The loco, which had entered service in 1936, was withdrawn in July 1964 and finally scrapped by Hayes at Bridgend.

Observed from the Mickleton Road at Honeybourne, an unidentified Grange 4-6-0 heads along the ex-Oxford, Worcester and Wolverhampton Railway route towards Oxford on a train from Worcester in 1961. It has just crossed over the now closed Birmingham Snow Hill to Cheltenham line at Honeybourne and is nearing the South Loop signal box. The massive water tower serving the numerous, I believe at least seven, water columns in the area can be seen above the train. Banking engines were stationed at Honeybourne to assist heavy goods trains along this section of line and up the long 1 in 100 bank to Chipping Campden tunnel. The track was singled in 1971 but double track has since been re-instated. It is now branded as the 'Cotswold Line'.

6977 GRUNDISBURGH HALL, allocated to Southall shed (81C), runs down Hatton Bank on a Southern Region bound express on Saturday 8 September 1962. This Modified Hall was built at Swindon in 1947 and was withdrawn, from Westbury (82D), in December 1963 and finally scrapped by Bird's at Newport.

An unidentified Hall is in charge of express V83 at Hatton on Saturday 8 September 1962. This was the Saturdays Only 10:04 from Margate which ran via Kensington Olympia and was due to arrive at Birmingham Snow Hill at 15:00. The first carriage is painted in the early British Railways livery of crimson lake and cream.

Oxley's (84B) 6917 OLDLANDS HALL leaves Stratford-upon-Avon towards Birmingham with what was probably a much needed banker in the Summer of 1963. The rusty rails to the right lead to the by then closed Ministry of Food cold store. The combined water tank and coaling stage on the shed approach road can be seen behind the locomotive. 6917 was built in 1941 and withdrawn in September 1965. Oxley depot was re-coded 2B in September 1963.

6870 BODICOTE GRANGE has just passed under the Shrewley Common road bridge near Hatton North Junction on Saturday 7 August 1965. This was train 1V32, the 10:45 Summer Saturdays Only Wolverhampton Low Level to Weymouth Town where it was due to arrive at 16:42. 6870, built in 1939, and allocated to Oxley shed (2B). It was withdrawn during the month after this photograph was taken and scrapped at Cashmore's of Great Bridge.

On Saturday 13 July 1963, Machynlleth (89C) allocated 7821 DITCHEAT MANOR leaves Aberystwyth in charge of the 09:45 'Cambrian Coast Express'. The castellated tower on the right was demolished in 1968. This is the site of Plas Crûg, otherwise known as Rheidol Castle. References to what was probably this castle go back to the twelfth century. There seems to be some dispute about the amount of original fortified building remaining as it had possibly been rebuilt as an eighteenth century folly with much of the site incorporated into a farmhouse. 7821 was built at Swindon by British Railways in 1950 and was withdrawn in November 1965. It was rescued from the famous Woodham Bros scrap line at Barry in 1980 and, after several moves to different preserved lines, it was restored and steamed on the West Somerset Railway. It has visited a number of other lines and it has recently been on display in Swindon.

7820 DINMORE MANOR attacks the Talerddig bank without assistance on the 'Cambrian Coast Express' on Monday 28 June 1965. This was the last year to see Manors in BR service on the line. The train had left Aberystwyth at 09:50 and joined the 08:20 Pwllheli portion at Dovey Junction and was due to arrive at London Paddington at 16:00. This locomotive was built at Swindon Works by British Railways in 1950 and it was withdrawn in November 1965, just five months after this photograph was taken. It is now preserved and based on the Gloucestershire Warwickshire Railway but has visited several other lines.

7822 FOXCOTE MANOR is seen near Llanbrynmair at the start of the eastbound Talerddig climb on Saturday 15 August 1964. This Summer Saturdays only 10:45 departure from Aberystwyth and 10:30 departure from Barmouth to Manchester Piccadilly (arrive 16:12) had combined at Dovey Junction. 7822 was allocated to Machynlleth (6F) at this time. Built at Swindon by British Railways in 1950 and withdrawn from service in November 1965, it is now preserved and, appropriately, based in Wales on the Llangollen Railway.

Carrying a Bristol Bath Road (82A) shed plate, 4-6-0 1000 COUNTY OF MIDDLESEX is seen leaving Stratford-upon-Avon on a westbound train in 1961. The headcode 1C85 indicates it was the 10:50 Summer Saturdays only Wolverhampton Low Level to Minehead and Ilfracombe which left Stratford at 12:04. The large water tower which dwarfed the West signal box by the Alcester Road bridge can be seen on the left. The locomotive was built in 1945 and it was withdrawn in July 1964 and cut up at the end of the year by Cashmore's at Newport.

Saturday 8 September 1962 and St Philips Marsh (82B) loco 1005, COUNTY OF DEVON, runs up the 1 in 105 Hatton Bank on train 1H18. This was the Saturdays Only 10:30 Weymouth to Wolverhampton Low Level, where it was due to arrive at 17:09. Built at Swindon in 1945, 1005 was withdrawn in June 1963 and scrapped fourteen months later by Cashmore's at Newport.

Ex-Great Western Railway Tender Engines
2: Local Passenger Services

Worcester (85A) allocated 7005 SIR EDWARD ELGAR, a single chimney Castle, was on the 08:32 departure from Stratford-upon-Avon to Birmingham Snow Hill (arrive 09:18) via Solihull on Saturday 4 July 1964. This service had started out from Worcester as a stopping train but the timetable encouraged catching a later express and changing to it at Evesham which it left at 08:00. 7005 entered service as LAMPHEY CASTLE in 1946 but was renamed after the composer in 1957. It was withdrawn in September 1964 and scrapped by Cohens at Morriston, near Swansea. The Collett 4,000 gallon tender is well stocked with coal.

Proudly showing off its double chimney, Tyseley's (2A) 7014 CAERHAYS CASTLE runs alongside Stratford racecourse on the 18:39 Evesham train on Thursday 25 June 1964. This service left Birmingham Snow Hill at 17:45 with the destination advertised as Worcester Shrub Hill until 1961. After this through passengers were transferred to the 'Cathedrals Express' at Evesham. 7014 was built in 1948, withdrawn February 1965 and cut up by Cashmore's at Great Bridge. The first carriage, M5988M, is an LMS designed 57ft corridor brake third (BTK).

Tyseley's (2A) Modified Hall 7908 HENSHALL HALL has just crossed the Stannels Bridge over the River Avon, near Stratford-upon-Avon, on the evening train to Evesham on Monday 20 July 1964. This section of line, from Stratford to Cheltenham Spa, was closed in 1976 except for the section from the ex-Ministry of Defence depot at Long Marston to Honeybourne. The trackbed between Stratford and Long Marston is now the Stratford Greenway cycling and walking path but there have been frequent suggestions that it should be re-opened for rail use. 7908 entered service in 1950 and was withdrawn in October 1965 and cut up at Cashmore's at Great Bridge soon afterwards.

5927 GUILD HALL has also crossed the Stannels Bridge over the River Avon on its way to Evesham. It had left Stratford station at 18:39 on Monday 11 May 1964. GUILD HALL was built in 1933 and was withdrawn from service, from Tyseley (2A), in October 1964 and scrapped by Cashmore's at Great Bridge. 'Stannel' is an old word for a Kestrel.

6806 BLACKWELL GRANGE from Worcester (85A), hurries by past a carpet of buttercups at Bishopton on the 08:32 departure from Stratford-upon-Avon to Birmingham Snow Hill on Saturday 16 May 1964. This locomotive was built in 1936 and withdrawn in October 1964. The first coach, W2227W, is a Frederick Hawksworth Great Western designed 64ft 4-compartment corridor brake third which was built by BR in 1950.

6861 CRYNANT GRANGE is seen in charge of the 18:39 departure from Stratford-upon-Avon to Evesham service on Friday 2 July 1964. It has passed the junction with the Stratford-upon-Avon and Midland Junction line to Fenny Compton and the racecourse platform and is running alongside Stratford racecourse. The spire of Holy Trinity church, where William Shakespeare is buried, can be seen in the distance behind the train. Built in 1939, 6861 was withdrawn, from Tyseley shed (2A), in October 1965 and scrapped by G Cohen at Kettering.

7812 ERLESTOKE MANOR pulls out of Oswestry station on the 11:25 Saturdays excepted all stations Oswestry to Whitchurch service while a DMU waits in the bay platform on the 11:45 to Gobowen on Tuesday 4 August 1964. It is interesting to note the complex layout and multiple platforms of this once important station which lost its through passenger services to Welshpool and beyond on 18 January 1965. A shuttle service to the main line at Gobowen continued until 7 November 1966 when the station was closed to passenger traffic. Cambrian Heritage Railways are working towards restoring the line from Oswestry to Gobowen and for some distance along the line south towards Pant. 7812 was built in 1939 and withdrawn in November 1965. It is now preserved on the Severn Valley Railway.

7829 RAMSBURY MANOR from Didcot (81E), passes by on Southern metals near Wokingham on the 12:37 departure from Guildford which was due to arrive at Reading Southern at 13:31 on Friday 1 January 1965. New Year's Day was not a public holiday in England at the time. This was just three days before diesel units were introduced on the line and steam haulage ceased. 7829 was built at Swindon by British Railways in 1950. It was withdrawn in December 1965 and scrapped by Cashmore's at Newport.

7814 FRINGFORD MANOR rolls along through pleasant countryside near Longhope on the 14:43 all stations departure from Hereford which was due to arrive at Gloucester Central at 15:58 on Saturday 8 August 1964. The line, opened in 1855 as broad gauge, closed on 2 November the same year as the photograph was taken. The locomotive had entered service in 1939 and was shedded at Gloucester Horton Road (85B) at the time. It was withdrawn in September 1965 and cut up by Bird's at Long Marston.

Mogul 7319 near Longhope on Saturday 8 August 1964 in charge of the Saturdays Only 14:47 departure from Gloucester Central which was due to arrive at Hereford at 16:17 after stopping at all stations along the now closed line via Ross-on-Wye. There were eight passenger trains a day in each direction on weekdays and Saturdays but no service on Sundays.

7319 again near Longhope on a Hereford train Saturday 8 August 1964. This Churchward designed 2-6-0 entered service in 1922 but it was withdrawn, from Gloucester Horton Road shed (85B), just two months after this photograph was taken. The first carriage, W2163W, is a Hawksworth designed 64ft Corridor Brake Third (BTK) with four compartments constructed by British Railways in 1950.

One of Collett's 2251 class 0-6-0s, 2210, leaves Stratford-upon-Avon from platform three on the two coach 08:43 local to Leamington Spa on Tuesday 13 August 1963. The lines through the gates on the right lead to the Ministry of Food cold store constructed during the Second World War. This is now the site of a Morrisons supermarket. 2210 was built in 1939, withdrawn in June 1965 and scrapped by Cashmore's at Great Bridge. Its home shed was Leamington Spa (84D) at the time this photograph was taken.

A few days later, on Saturday 17 August 1963, 2210 was on the 08:43 local to Leamington Spa again as it neared the bridge over the Stratford-upon-Avon Canal and Stratford East signal box. The leading coach, composite first & third class brake corridor SC21017, was far from home! The signal box, too, had travelled as the structure was originally sited at Acton West and had been reconstructed at Stratford sometime around 1933.

Ex-Great Western Railway Tender Engines
3: Delivering the Goods

6813 EASTBURY GRANGE, from Ebbw Junction (86A), is seen passing through Gloucester Central station on a class H goods train on Saturday 1 February 1964. A rebuilt GWR Syphon G parcels van marked 'To Work Between Paddington and Gloucester' is at the rear of the train on the opposite platform. 6813 was built in 1936 and withdrawn, from Worcester (85A), in September 1965. It was cut up at Bird's Long Marston.

6826 NANNERTH GRANGE rounds the 'new' curve at Stratford-upon-Avon on a train of loaded iron ore tippler wagons heading for South Wales. 6834 DUMMER GRANGE is passing on the up line hauling a train of sheeted loaded wagons in the early afternoon of Wednesday 11 March 1964. The opening of this curve in 1960 meant that iron ore trains to South Wales from quarries including Oxfordshire Ironstone near Banbury, plus other trains via Woodford Halse, could use this more direct route. Trains had previously run along the, by this time closed, section of the Stratford-upon-Avon and Midland Junction Railway (SMJ) line from Stratford to Broom Junction. 6826 was withdrawn in May 1965 and 6834 in June 1964.

6874 HAUGHTON GRANGE passes through Stratford's wooden sleeper built Racecourse Platform on a goods train on a glorious Monday 11 May 1964. The abutments of the demolished bridge on the closed Stratford-upon-Avon and Midland Junction Railway (SMJ) line to Broom Junction can be seen at the end. The 'new' curve, which made it redundant, is on the right. This very basic platform was opened on 6 May 1933 for use on race days. It was closed in 1968. Oxford (81F) shedded 6874 was built in 1939, withdrawn in September 1965 and scrapped at Cashmore's of Great Bridge.

6834 DUMMER GRANGE has pulled out of the North Goods Yard to join the main line and cross the bridge over Grange Road into Knowle & Dorridge station. The train is loaded with Austin 1100 saloon cars from the Longbridge works on Monday 27 April 1964. The BMC colour 'Old English White' seems to have been popular! Built in 1937 and withdrawn from Tyseley (2A) in June 1964, just two months after this photograph was taken, 6834 was cut up at Cashmore's of Great Bridge.

7814 FRINGFORD MANOR waits on the middle line at Gloucester Central station while 5939 TANGLEY HALL approaches on Monday 10 August 1964. A class 123 diesel multiple unit has just departed on the 17:20 from Cardiff General to Derby which had left on time at 18:32. 7814 entered service at the beginning of 1939. At the time of the photograph it was allocated to Horton Road shed (85B) and was withdrawn from there in September 1965 and later scrapped at Bird's Long Marston. 5939 was built in 1933 and withdrawn, from Newport Ebbw Junction (86B), in October 1964 and scrapped at Hay's, Bridgend.

7802 BRADLEY MANOR passes by on the scenic single track line running along the wall by the River Dyfi (Dovey) estuary near Fron-Goch, between Aberdyfi (Aberdovey) and Dovey Junction, on Monday 28 June 1965. This was the afternoon pick-up goods train from Pwllheli to Machynlleth. The two Great Western Fruit 'D' vans were possibly being used as parcels vans or for returning empty Central Dairies milk crates to Newtown. The red bracket on the tender front prevented fire irons coming into contact with the overhead electric wires. See 7801 on page 68 for instance. 7802 was built at Swindon Works in 1938 and withdrawn in November 1965. After spending some time in the Woodham Bros scrapyard at Barry it was bought for preservation and it is now based on the Severn Valley Railway.

Modified Hall 7916 MOBBERLEY HALL has just crossed the canal bridge on a northbound fitted freight at Stratford-upon-Avon on Saturday 17 August 1963. I believe this was train 5M44, the Marazion (Penzance) to Crewe perishable goods train which was at times hauled by a Castle. It had earlier been scheduled to leave Marazion daily at 17:05 but the 1963 working timetable showed it as starting at Tavistock Junction, Plymouth, at 21:35 on Fridays arriving at Stratford and taking on water at 07:42 the following morning. It only started from Penzance on Wednesdays.

7916 MOBBERLEY HALL pulls away from Stratford-upon-Avon on its northbound fitted freight on Saturday 17 August 1963. The first wagon is a BR Conflat A with two Conflat A containers. 7916 was shedded at the time at Plymouth Laira (83D), lending support to it being train 5M44 bound for Crewe. It was built in 1950 and withdrawn in December 1964. It was cut up at Swindon.

Modified Hall 6999 CAPEL DEWI HALL was nearing its end, minus its nameplates, when climbing Hatton Bank on the slow line on an unfitted goods train just before midday on Sunday 19 September 1965. 6999 had entered service in 1949. It was withdrawn, from Oxford shed (81F), three months after this photograph was taken, and cut up by Cashmore's at Newport.

Oxford's (81F) 5955 GARTH HALL passes Gloucester Horton Road shed (85B) on a train of standard BR mineral wagons carrying coal on Saturday 1 February 1964. 5955 was built in 1935 and withdrawn in April 1965. This locomotive was converted to oil burning and renumbered 3950 in 1946 but it was restored to coal burning two years later. The photograph was taken from the level crossing where Horton Road becomes Derby Road and at the start of Tramway Junction where the lines to the right of the picture run to Cheltenham and to the left to Bristol and beyond.

3217 is hard at work banking a goods train headed by 6804 BROCKINGTON GRANGE at Bishopton, the start of the 1 in 75 Wilmcote Bank, on Saturday 20 June 1964. The new Stratford-upon-Avon Parkway station has now been built near here. Bringing up the rear of the train is ex-LNER Toad D 20-ton brake van E226133 next to a BR standard steel ended plywood body 12-ton van labelled ICI fertilizer. 3217 entered service in 1947 and was withdrawn in November 1964.

An undignified duty for a once proud express locomotive, 5091 CLEEVE ABBEY on an unfitted coal train from the Forest of Dean approaches Over Junction on Saturday 15 February 1964 just three months before the line, opened by the Ledbury and Gloucester Railway in 1885, was closed on 30 May. Passenger services had already ceased in 1959 but the Dymock to Gloucester section remained open for goods. Apparently, in its heyday the route was known by locals as the Daffodil Line. 5091 entered service as Star class locomotive 4071 in 1923 and was rebuilt as a Castle in 1938. It was withdrawn in October 1964 and scrapped soon after at Cashmore's of Great Bridge.

'Night Owl' 4707 from Southall (81C) is unusually active during the day on a northbound express freight at Hatton on Saturday 8 September 1962. This was one of a small class of nine 2-8-0 mixed traffic locomotives designed by Churchward. They were mainly used on overnight express goods trains but also, at times, on Summer relief passenger trains. 4707 was built at Swindon Works in 1923 and withdrawn in May 1964. The line on the right allowed slow goods trains to be overtaken while climbing Hatton Bank.

A very unkempt Churchward designed ex-GWR Mogul 2-6-0, 6349, passes over the kissing gate protected Shottery Fields footpath at Stratford-upon-Avon on a train of standard BR mineral wagons in the late Autumn sunshine on Saturday 16 November 1963. This was six days before President Kennedy was assassinated in Dallas. Built in 1923 and withdrawn in August 1964, 6349 was shedded at Gloucester Horton Road (85B) at the time of the photograph.

This was the atmosphere of much of latter day steam in Britain. A grimy, leaking 5330 clanks past Gloucester Horton Road crossing on an unfitted freight on Saturday 4 January 1964. Built in 1917, it was shedded at the time at Horton Road (85B) but was transferred at the end of month to Didcot (81E) where it was withdrawn the following June.

On one of its very last duties, Churchward designed 2800 class 2857 has just passed through Mountain Ash Cardiff Road station travelling in the Pontypool Road direction on a long partly-fitted express goods train of box vans on Saturday 6 April 1963. The houses are Cresselly Villas on the Cardiff Road. This ex-Vale of Neath Railway line is now closed and trains use the ex-Taff Vale line on the other side of the Afon Cynon. The locomotive was built at Swindon Works in 1918 and withdrawn, from Neath Court Sart shed (87A), later in the same month. After some time in the scrap line at Woodham's at Barry it was bought for preservation and restored. It is now to be found at the Severn Valley Railway.

Collett 2884 class, a development of the 2800 class easily identified because of a cab-side window, 3812 is seen on a train of BR standard mineral wagons carrying iron ore bound for South Wales. It is just about to join the former GWR Stratford to Honeybourne route next to the Stratford-upon-Avon Racecourse platform on the 'new' curve linking it with the former Stratford and Midland Junction Railway on Thursday 2 July 1964. Newport Ebbw Junction (86B) allocated 3812 was built in 1939 and withdrawn in June 1965 and scrapped. Church Farm is to the right of the locomotive and the Old Town engine shed water tower, which survived the demolition of the other buildings as it continued to supply water for the iron ore trains, can just be seen on the far right.

3816 of Severn Tunnel Junction (86E), missing its smokebox number plate, heads a mixed freight train of mineral wagons and box vans past Clifford Sidings signal box on the former Stratford-upon-Avon and Midland Junction Railway on its way to Oxfordshire on Saturday 23 January 1965. This was just five weeks before the last freight workings on the line. 3816 was built in 1940 and withdrawn in July 1965.

Ex-Great Western Railway Tender Engines
4: On Shed and at the Works

Showing the quality of Swindon's paintwork, Modified Hall, 6961 STEDHAM HALL, from Old Oak Common (81A), could almost have been used as a shaving mirror at the Works on Sunday 7 April 1963. It entered service in 1944 and was withdrawn in September 1965 and cut up by Cashmore's at Newport two months later. The tender is a Hawksworth flat sided 4,000 gallon type.

Craven Arms, a sub-shed of Shrewsbury (89A), was situated on the ex-LNWR's Central Wales Line from Shrewsbury to Carmarthen. 2242 stands there alongside BR standard class 5 4-6-0 73003 on Sunday 14 July 1963. 73003, allocated at the time to Shrewsbury shed, was built at Derby Works in 1951 and was withdrawn for scrapping in December 1965. 2242 was allocated to Hereford (85C). Built in 1945, it was withdrawn in May 1965 and scrapped soon afterwards. The shed closed in May 1964 but the line is still in operation.

2295 and 6810 BLAKEMERE GRANGE stand alongside each other on Hereford shed (85C) on Sunday 4 March 1962. 2295, at its home shed, was built at Swindon in 1938 and withdrawn in October 1962. Pontypool Road (86G) allocated Grange 6810 was built at Swindon in 1936 and withdrawn in October 1964 and scrapped by Bird's at Bridgend.

Railway Walk, Worcester, was a marvellous vantage point used by many photographers over the years. Double chimney Castle class 4-6-0 7007 GREAT WESTERN, bearing the company crest on the splasher below the nameplate, moves towards Worcester shed (85A) in August 1962. There is an interesting collection of ex-GWR single and twin-coupled diesel railcars in the yard. Built in 1946 and named OGMORE CASTLE for the first eighteen months, 7007 was the last of the class to be built by the GWR. The remainder were built by British Railways after Nationalisation. It was withdrawn during February 1963 and scrapped by Cashmore's at Great Bridge.

Old Oak Common's (81A) double chimney Castle 5057 EARL WALDEGRAVE waits in steam near the coaling stage at Gloucester Horton Road shed (85B) during April 1963. Built in 1936, it carried the name PENRICE CASTLE for a year before being renamed after one of the Great Western Railway directors. It was withdrawn in March 1964, after working for just over one and a quarter million miles in service, and scrapped at Swindon.

The 1950 built 7029 CLUN CASTLE was withdrawn from Gloucester Horton Road (85B), at the very end of steam on the Western Region in December 1965. Fortunately it was purchased for preservation and is seen here on the Banbury shed (2D) turntable on Thursday 12 May 1966. It is now based at the Tyseley Locomotive Works. Although originally a Western shed coded 84C, Banbury had been transferred to the London Midland in September 1963. It was closed to steam in October 1966.

6011 KING JAMES I awaits its fate minus its tender back home at Swindon Works, where it had been constructed in 1930, on Sunday 7 April 1963. All thirty examples of the King class were withdrawn during 1962 and 6011 had been taken out of service in the December. It was scrapped during January 1964. These 8P power classified locomotives were built to slightly larger proportions and weight than normal. This was made possible by the generous dimensions of the Brunel designed 7 ft $1/4$ in gauge GWR routes. The double red discs that can be seen above the number plate indicate the resultant restricted range of these locomotives.

Collett designed 4-6-0 7801 ANTHONY MANOR rests on its home depot, Oswestry (89D), on Thursday 17 August 1961. It was built at Swindon Works in 1938 and withdrawn in July 1965 and scrapped at Bird's, Swansea. These light locomotives were particularly suitable for hauling trains on the former Cambrian Railways main lines.

7800 TORQUAY MANOR and 7827 LYDHAM MANOR at Aberystwyth main line shed on Saturday 13 July 1963. Note that 7800 is sporting overhead live wires warning signs. This was possibly in preparation for its imminent transfer to the London Midland Region but more likely because, at the time of the photograph, it could have found itself under the newly installed wires at Crewe as it was allocated to Shrewsbury shed (89A). 7827, one of the later British Railways built batch of Manors, was shedded at Oswestry (89D). Aberystwyth was a sub-shed of Machynlleth (89C). The first of its class, 7800 was built in 1938 and withdrawn in August 1964 and then scrapped by Cashmore's at Great Bridge.

3823 of Oxford (81F) shed looks very smart and possibly ex-works on Gloucester Horton Road shed (85B) during April 1963. Although basically a Churchward 1903 designed 2-8-0, 3823 was one of the later locomotives with Collett modifications built at Swindon Works in 1940. It was withdrawn in July 1965 and cut up by Bird's at Long Marston. The large Horton Road gasworks gasholder looms over the shed.

2251 class 3217, a Leamington Spa (84D) allocated locomotive, waits for duty in the sunshine in the goods loop near the goods yard approach and the by then closed engine shed at Stratford-upon-Avon on Friday 5 July 1963. Built in 1947, it was withdrawn from Leamington in November 1964 and cut up the following month at Cashmore's of Great Bridge.

Ex-Great Western Railway Tender Engines
5: Excursion Trains and Enthusiast Specials

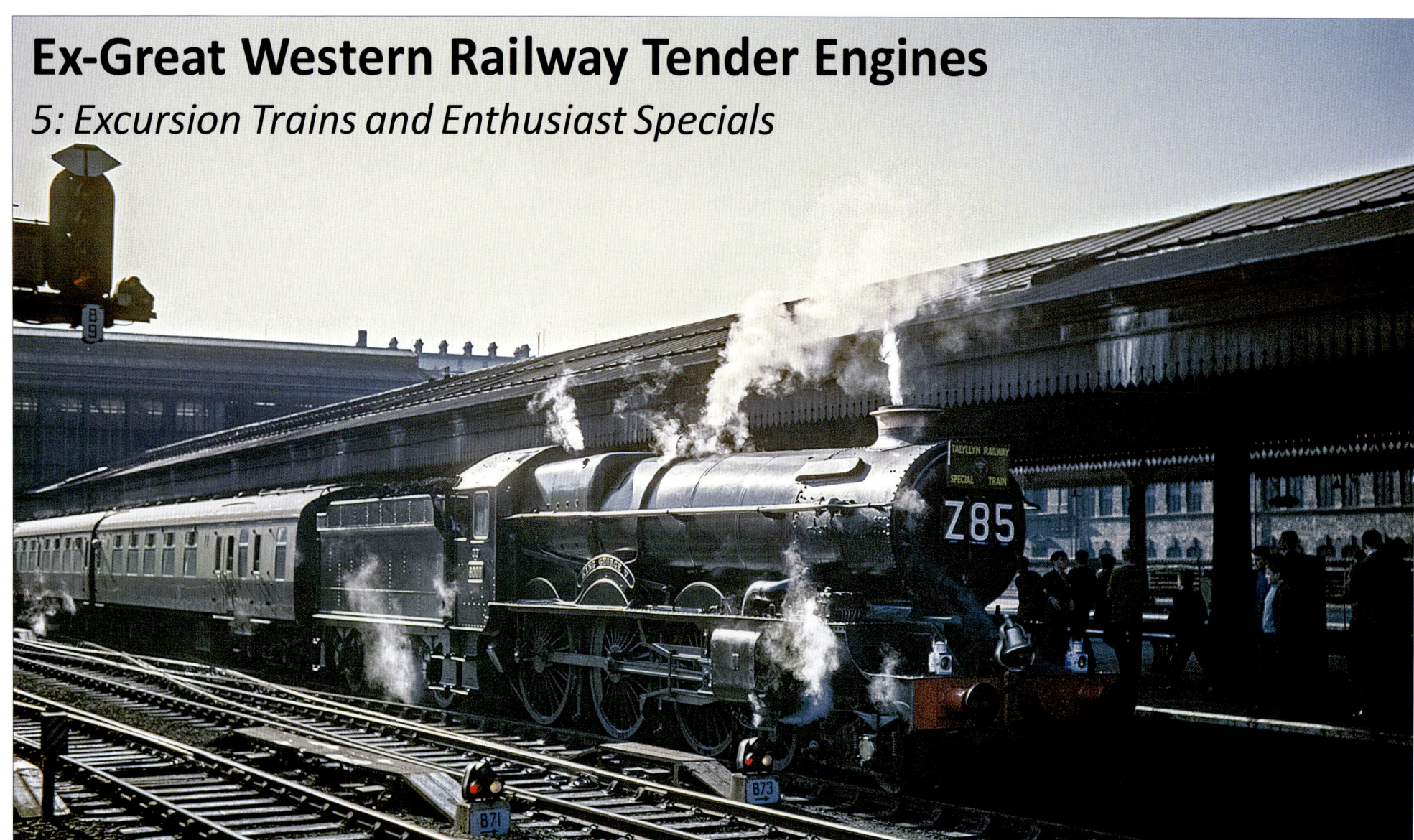

6000 KING GEORGE V on the Talyllyn Railway Preservation Society 10th Special Train at Birmingham Snow Hill mid-morning on Saturday 29 September 1962. 6000 was in charge of the train from Paddington to Ruabon where 7801 ANTHONY MANOR and 7314 took over for the rest of the route via Llangollen to Towyn (now Tywyn). I caught this train at Snow Hill which involved an overnight journey back via Welshpool. The bell that was presented to the locomotive by the Baltimore and Ohio Railroad Company during its visit to the USA in 1927 can clearly be seen. 6000 was built in 1927 and officially withdrawn in December 1962 but it is now preserved as part of the National Collection.

As mentioned previously 7801 ANTHONY MANOR and 7314 took over this Special train at Ruabon station. They were in charge for the rest of the journey through Llangollen, Corwen and Dolgelly (Dolgellau in Welsh) joining the Machynlleth to Pwllheli line at Morfa Mawddach. 7314 was built in 1921 and withdrawn in February 1963. This station is still in use on the ex-Great Western line between Wrexham and Shrewsbury and it is sometimes cited as the ideal, if probably impossible to achieve, mainline connection with the preserved Llangollen Railway.

7801 ANTHONY MANOR, double headed with the unseen 7314, stops at Corwen on the Talyllyn Railway Preservation Society special on Saturday 29 September 1962. The Ruabon to Morfa Mawddach line was officially closed to passengers on 18 January 1965 although flooding meant that some sections were closed the previous month. This ex GWR station, which opened in 1865, is now in private hands but a new one, Corwen Central, has been built by the preserved Llangollen Railway as the terminus of its extension to the town. ANTHONY MANOR, built in 1938, was withdrawn in July 1965.

Two years later 7029 CLUN CASTLE is seen at Wolverhampton Low Level station on the 1964 Talyllyn Railway Ian Allan Limited special train on Saturday 26 September. It had brought the train from Paddington but was replaced at Wolverhampton handing over to 1011 COUNTY OF CHESTER which hauled the train as far as Ruabon where 7827 LYDHAM MANOR and then by the preserved 'Small Prairie' 4555 took over for the rest of the run on to Morfa Mawddach and Towyn for the society's AGM.

7827 LYDHAM MANOR and 'Small Prairie' 4555 have arrived at Towyn (Tywyn) on the Tallyllyn Railway special on Saturday 26 September 1964. They had hauled the train from Ruabon via Dolgelly (Dolgellau) and Morfa Mawddach just a few months before the closure of that line. 7827 entered service at the end of 1950 and was withdrawn in October 1965. Acquired by Woodham's, Barry, in May 1966, it was sold to the Dart Valley Railway and left as the fifth departure from Barry in June 1970. Since restoration it has been on loan to several other heritage railways. As in 1962, the return was overnight via Welshpool. I was also on this special: another long, but very enjoyable and memorable, day.

5054 EARL OF DUCIE near Honeybourne on the Oxford University Railway Society 'Castle Farewell' special on Saturday 16 May 1964. It was said to be doing 92 mph hauling its seven coaches at this point. The train had started at Paddington and was on its way from Oxford to Worcester and then to Hereford. From there it would return to Paddington via Pontypool Road, Severn Tunnel Junction and Swindon. 5054 was built in 1936 and withdrawn in October 1964. It was briefly named LAMPHEY CASTLE until the name of one of the GWR directors was transferred to it from Dukedog 3211 in 1937. At the time of the photograph it was attached to a Hawksworth flat sided 4,000 gallon tender.

7023 PENRICE CASTLE from Worcester shed (85A), has just taken over from 44558 and 53807 at Bath Green Park station on the Home Counties Railway Society 'Somerset & Dorset Railtour' on Sunday 7 June 1964. The tour ran from Waterloo to Paddington via Southampton, Bournemouth Central, Evercreech Junction, Bath Green Park, Gloucester Eastgate and Swindon. 35005 and 7025 were also involved. 7023 was built by British Railways in 1949 and withdrawn in February 1965 from Oxley shed (2A). The station's impressive vaulted glass roof, partly damaged by wartime bombing, can be seen behind the train. The last passenger service left in 1966 and as a grade II listed building it is now used as a market, retail and entertainments venue.

Single chimney Castle 4079 PENDENNIS CASTLE looks in excellent condition near Kemble on Sunday 8 August 1965 on an Ian Allan railtour which ran as 1Z40 from Paddington to Worcester Shrub Hill via Oxford, returning via Cheltenham and Swindon. The locomotive, famous for its part in the locomotive exchange trials with the LNER in 1925, was built at Swindon Works in 1924 and withdrawn in May 1964 after running for just over one and three quarter million miles in service. It was bought for preservation but in 1977 was sold to the Hamersley Iron Pty Ltd in Western Australia where it hauled tourist trains on their extensive network. It was repatriated in 2000 and is now based at the Didcot Railway Centre.

Churchward Mogul 6368 and Collett 0-6-0 2246 wait at the ex-Stratford-upon-Avon and Midland Junction Railway Stratford Old Town station on the 'Thames, Severn and Avon Railtour' on Saturday 12 October 1963. The ambitious itinerary was from Waterloo to Paddington via Weybridge, Reading General, Oxford, Banbury, Woodford Halse, Stratford-upon-Avon Old Town, Honeybourne, Worcester Shrub Hill, Bromsgrove, Birmingham New Street, Bromsgrove, Cheltenham Spa Lansdown Road, Gloucester South Junction, Kemble and Swindon. As well as 2246 and 6368, 7005, 30120, 31790, 45552, 82023 and 92223 were involved on this tour.

The 'Thames, Severn and Avon Railtour' at Stratford-upon-Avon Old Town station. 6368 was built in 1925 and 2246 in 1945. Both were withdrawn two months after this excursion, in December 1963. The large government grain silo which was built next to Lucy and Nephew's Mill during the Second World War has since been demolished. Both the silo and the mill had previously been rail connected. The spire of Holy Trinity Church, where William Shakespeare is buried, surveys the scene which is now the site of a housing estate. Also of interest is the grounded carriage and the long disused East and West Junction Railway (a forerunner of the SMJR) wooden signal box.

In the days when Health and Safety were of less concern, 1011 COUNTY OF CHESTER on the Stephenson Locomotive Society 'Farewell to the GWR County Class Railtour' pauses for water at Gloucester South Junction on Sunday 20 September 1964. It had started from Birmingham Snow Hill and ran via Gloucester South Junction to Swindon Works and then returned to Birmingham via Oxford and Banbury.

1011 COUNTY OF CHESTER waits while the passengers visit Swindon Works on the same tour. 1011 was allocated to Swindon (82C) at the time. It had entered service in 1946 and it was withdrawn in November 1964 and cut up the following March by Cashmore's at Newport.

Hall class 6915 MURSLEY HALL leaves Stratford-upon-Avon towards Birmingham on a special excursion at 18:40 on Thursday 9 July 1964. This locomotive, which entered service in 1941, was allocated to Shrewsbury shed (6D) at the time and was withdrawn from Banbury depot (2D), in February 1965. The passengers had probably been treated to a matinee performance of Richard II with David Warner in the title role at the Royal Shakespeare Theatre. There were several special trains in 1964 as part of the Shakespeare quatercentenary celebrations.

Ex-Great Western Railway Railway Tank Engines
6: Saddle Tanks

Ex-GWR 1361 class 0-6-0ST 1363 on the coaling stage ramp at Plymouth Laira shed (83D) on Saturday 26 August 1961. It was one of a small class of five Churchward designed short wheelbase outside cylinder dock shunters. 1363 was built at Swindon in 1910 and withdrawn in November 1962. It was bought for preservation by members of the Great Western Society and is now based at the Didcot Railway Centre. The Laira coaling stage was unusual because locomotives could be loaded from both sides.

1361 class 1365 oozes steam alongside 5943 ELMDON HALL at Bristol St Philip's Marsh shed (82B) on Friday 25 August 1961. 1365 was, like 1363, built at Swindon in 1910 and withdrawn in November 1962 but it was cut up at Cashmore's Newport ten months later. The shed closed to steam in June 1964 and it is now the site of the Bristol Wholesale Fruit Centre.

1152 awaits its fate with coupling rods removed at Swansea Danygraig shed (87C) on Sunday 12 August 1962. It was a Peckett & Co. of Bristol E class 0-4-0ST built for Powlesland & Mason in 1912 (works number 1179) as No.12 in their fleet. It became GWR 935 and later BR 1152. It was withdrawn in December 1961.

Another Peckett E class 0-4-0ST, 1151, is seen still in service at Swansea East Dock shed (87D) on Monday 13 August 1962. It was built for Powlesland & Mason in 1916 (works number 1449) as No.4 in their fleet and it became GWR 779 and later BR 1151. It was withdrawn in August 1964 and cut up seven months later.

1338 waits for work at Swansea East Dock shed (87D) on Monday 13 August 1962. It was built by Kitson of Leeds in 1898 (works number 3799) as one of a pair of 0-4-0 saddle tanks for the Cardiff Railway which were absorbed into the GWR at the grouping in 1923. Cardiff Railways No.5 became 1338 and outlived its sister, No.6 renumbered 1339 by the GWR which had been scrapped in 1934, in regular service by nearly thirty years.

1338 was withdrawn by BR in September 1963 and was saved for preservation and displayed at the Yieldingtree Railway Museum at the already closed Bleadon and Uphill station, near Weston-super-Mare. Seen here on Thursday 3 March 1966, it moved on to the Didcot Railway Centre in 1987 and was restored to working order in GWR livery.

Another South Wales 0-4-0 saddle tank, and one which was never a BR locomotive, was 1340 TROJAN. It is seen here out of steam at Alders Paper Mill at Tamworth on Sunday 24 March 1963. It was built by the Avonside Engine Co in 1897 (works number 1386) and belonged to Messrs Dunn & Shute of Newport Town Dock until, in 1903, it was purchased by the Alexandra Docks Railway, Newport, which was then absorbed into the GWR at the railway grouping in 1923. Sold to the Netherseal Colliery, Burton-on-Trent, in July 1932, it was re-sold to Alders in 1947. Amazingly, it retained its GWR number plates. Now preserved in GWR livery, TROJAN has been based at the Didcot Railway Centre since 1968.

Ex-Great Western Railway Tank Engines
7: 5700 type 0-6-0 Pannier Tanks

Collett designed Ex-GWR 5700 class 0-6-0 pannier tank 3754 on pilot duty at Paddington station in August 1960. It was shedded at Old Oak Common (81A) and this diagram was mainly to bring in or take out empty stock for main line trains. 3754 was built at Swindon in 1937 and withdrawn, from Shrewsbury shed (6D), in November 1965. It was scrapped at Cashmore's of Great Bridge.

9705 is in steam at Old Oak Common shed (81A) in 1961. It was built at Swindon in 1933 as one of a 5700 sub-class of eleven 0-6-0PT locomotives fitted with condensing equipment for underground working. The external pipework and steam exhaust can be seen in front of the dome. They were allocated to Old Oak Common and mainly used on the Hammersmith & City and Metropolitan lines between Paddington and Smithfield Meat Market although they were sometimes seen on Paddington station pilot duty during the day. 9705 was withdrawn later in the year this photograph was taken, in October 1961.

Abercynon's (88E) 8717 waits for service at Llantrisant shed (88G) on Saturday 6 April 1963, just ten days after Dr Beeching's 'The Reshaping of British Railways' was published. This 0-6-0PT was built for the GWR in 1931 as one of a lot of twenty-five by Beyer Peacock Ltd of Manchester. It was withdrawn in July 1964. The shed closed in October 1964.

9665 rests at its home shed, Hereford (85C), on Sunday 4 March 1962 with 5952 COGAN HALL alongside and 6876 KINGSLAND GRANGE in the distance beside the coaling stage. 9665 was built at Swindon in 1948 and withdrawn in February 1963. The shed closed to steam at the end of November 1964 and its site and that of the adjacent Barton goods yard is now host to a Sainsbury's supermarket, car park and Travelodge.

Pontypool Road (86G) allocated 0-6-0PT 3708 pulls away on a local passenger train on Saturday 6 April 1963 from Mountain Ash Cardiff Road station towards Aberdare past the now demolished Allen's Arms hotel, today the site of a car park. Originally the Vale of Neath Railway, this ex-Great Western line is now closed and lifted. The lines to the right ran to the Deep Dyffryn colliery. There was also a Taff Vale line Oxford Street station separated from the GWR one by the Afon Cynon.

3708 was still active two years later and it is seen here passing Pontypool Road Station South signal box on Monday 12 April 1965. The shunter is ready with his pole on the GWR shunters truck just behind the locomotive. This large GWR signal box was closed in 1979 and a road now covers the site. Built at Swindon in 1936, 3708 was, it seems, officially withdrawn in February 1965 but it was clearly back in action two months later! It was withdrawn a second time in the August and it met its end at Cashmore's, Newport, in October 1965.

4691 is in the company of 41243, 75072, 3210 and others on Templecombe shed (82G) on Sunday 7 June 1964. The curve on the left led to the ex-LSWR line in the Salisbury direction. The shed, along with the Somerset and Dorset Joint Railway line, was closed in 1966 and it is now the site of the UK headquarters of Thales Underwater Systems. The photograph was taken from a Home Counties Railway Society S&D special hauled on that section by 44558 and 53807. The train ran from Waterloo to Bournemouth Central and then along the S&D to Evercreech Junction, Highbridge and Bath Green Park. It then continued to Gloucester Eastgate and Paddington using a range of motive power. 4691 entered service in 1945 and was withdrawn in September 1964.

9600 stands in steam at NCB Merthyr Vale Colliery on Monday 30 December 1968. Despite its clean BR appearance with number plates and lion and wheel totem on the tank side, this was almost three years after the last use of regular steam on the Western Region and four months after the famous 'Fifteen Guinea Special' marking the end of its use on any BR region, with the notable exception of the three Vale of Rheidol locomotives. 9600 had been sold to the NCB in October 1965 after it was withdrawn from BR service.

9600 is seen working hard in bright Winter sunshine at NCB Merthyr Vale Colliery on Monday 30 December 1968. When this 1945 Swindon built locomotive was withdrawn in turn by the NCB, in 1973, it was bought for preservation and is now to be found at the Standard Gauge Steam Trust at the Tyseley Locomotive Works in Birmingham. Aberfan is on the other side of the River Taff. This was the site of the terrible disaster caused by Merthyr Vale slag heaps on 21 October 1966. The colliery closed on 25 August 1989.

9792 is busy on duty at NCB Mardy (Maerdy in Welsh) Colliery on 27 August 1969 sporting authentic looking replica number and shed plates prepared by Mike Collins. It was built at Swindon in 1936 and it seems it spent its entire BR working life at Neath Court Sart shed (87A). When withdrawn by BR in March 1964 it went to the NCB Aberaman Railways but was transferred to Mardy Colliery the following year. There it was given the name MARDY No.4 and this had been painted on the cabside, along with 9792, where the original GWR number plate should have been. Sadly, unlike many other post BR survivors, it was not preserved and it was scrapped in September 1973.

7754 crosses the Afon Cynon at Mountain Ash Colliery on Wednesday 21 October 1970. It was built for the GWR by the North British Locomotive Company in 1930 (works number 24042) and was withdrawn by BR and sold to the NCB for use at Windsor Colliery in 1959. After moves to Llanbradach, Ogilvie, Elliot and Talywain it had been transferred to Mountain Ash five months before this photograph was taken. 7754 continued to work for another five years and, after another five years in store, it was presented by the NCB to the National Museum of Wales. It is now owned by the Llangollen Railway Trust. The church is St Margaret's in Dyffryn Road.

Ex-GWR 0-6-0PT L90 runs along London Underground tracks in charge of a short train to Croxley Tip on Thursday 31 July 1969. This was a load mainly of old sleepers sandwiched between two 20-ton brake vans, B556 and B557, built by Hurst Nelson & Co of Motherwell in 1935. B557, nearest the locomotive, is now preserved at the Buckinghamshire Railway Centre. L90 was one of a number of 5700 class pannier tanks used on engineering and other non-passenger trains.

After running round and taking on water at Watford, LTE L90 now faces chimney first to continue on the short run to Croxley Tip on Thursday 31 July 1969. This locomotive was built as GWR 7760 in 1930 as one of one hundred of the class constructed by the North British Locomotive Company of Glasgow. When it was withdrawn by BR in December 1961 it was transferred to the London Transport Executive where it became L90. Service with the LTE ended in 1971 and 7760 was bought for preservation and is now to be found at the Tyseley Locomotive Works in Birmingham.

Ex-Great Western Railway Tank Engines
8: Other classes of Pannier Tank

1503 brings empty stock into Paddington station on Sunday 7 July 1963. The 1500 class were 0-6-0 pannier tank locomotives designed by Hawksworth for the GWR but, following nationalisation in 1948, they were actually built at Swindon by the Western Region of British Railways the following year. Intended for heavy shunting duties, only ten of the type were built. 1503 was withdrawn in December 1963. The carriage is BR Mk1 57ft Full Brake (BG) M80597.

1509 built in 1949 spent its working life in South Wales, at Newport Pill (86B) and Ebbw Junction (86A) sheds, before being withdrawn by BR in August 1959. It was then sold, along with 1501 and 1502, to the NCB for use at Coventry, Keresley, Colliery where it is seen here on Monday 9 August 1965. When no longer required by the NCB, all three locomotives went to the Severn Valley Railway (SVR) where 1501 is still based. Unfortunately, 1502 and 1509 were used solely to provide spares for the restoration of 1501 and the remaining parts were scrapped at Cashmore's of Great Bridge in October 1970. Keresley Colliery began operating in 1917. It was closed in 1991 but was later reopened for a couple of years before finally closing in 1996.

1639 in Worcester shed yard (85A) is seen from the vantage point of Railway Walk in August 1962. The shed was situated in the triangle formed by the Great Western line, with Worcester Works on the other side, the MR line out of sight near the camera and a connecting loop which ran behind it. There is a BR class 4 4-6-0 in front of the shed. 1639 was built in 1951 and withdrawn, from Worcester, in November 1964.

The crew of 6435 fill the tanks with water at Yeovil Junction station in preparation for the 15:50 four minute run to Yeovil Town station on Wednesday 8 April 1964. Yeovil Junction station was opened by the London and South Western Railway (LSWR) in 1860 on its London to Exeter main line. Because it was situated some 1¾ miles from Yeovil there was a regular shuttle service to the town with two auto coaches which the locomotive could either pull or push. 6435 was built at Swindon works in 1937 as one of forty 6400 class pannier tanks designed by Charles Collett and introduced in 1932. It was withdrawn by BR in October 1964 but was bought for preservation and can now be found on the Bodmin & Wenford Railway in Cornwall.

Stourbridge Junction (2A) allocated 6434 prepares to leave its single carriage auto train at Dudley station on Saturday 2 May 1964. It had completed the only passenger turn on a Saturday along the 3¾ mile branch to Old Hill which had left Dudley at 12:26, arrived at Old Hill at 12:40 and left there at 12:45 to arrive back at Dudley at 12:59. The Old Hill service ended the following month. 6434 was built at Swindon works in 1937 and was withdrawn in September 1964. The station closed to all regular passenger services on 6 July 1964 and then became the site of the now closed Dudley Freightliner Terminal.

9437 looks resplendent and has obviously just been outshopped at Swindon Works on Sunday 7 April 1963. This Cardiff East Dock (88L) allocated Hawksworth GWR designed 9400 class 0-6-0PT was built for BR by Robert Stephenson & Hawthorns Ltd and entered service in 1951. It was withdrawn in June 1965 after spending its entire working life in South Wales.

Pontypool Road's (86G) 8495 nears Hafodyrynys on a local passenger train on Saturday 6 April 1963. It was, like 9437, built by Robert Stephenson and Hawthorns and it was delivered in 1952. It was withdrawn in November 1964. There was a platform at Hafodyrynys on the now closed line where some trains stopped on weekdays only. The last regular passenger train from Pontypool Road to Aberdare High Level ran on 13 June 1964.

9406 hauls empty stock out of Paddington station on Sunday 7 June 1964. Built at Swindon Works in 1947, 9406 was one of only ten of the 210 strong class to be built there. The rest were built by Robert Stephenson & Hawthorns Ltd, W G Bagnall and the Yorkshire Engine Company. 9406 was withdrawn in September 1964.

9405 has brought the empty stock for a main line express into platform two under the impressive wrought iron glazed Brunel roof at Paddington station on Saturday 19 September 1964. Built at Swindon in 1947, 9405 was withdrawn in June 1965.

Right. Ex-Barry Railway F class 138 pokes out of the shed at NCB Hafodyrynys Colliery on Saturday 6 April 1963. It was built by Hudswell Clarke in 1905 as an 0-6-0 saddle tank with the works number 717. It became GWR 780 and was rebuilt with pannier tanks at Swindon in 1927. It was sold in May 1936 to Burnyeats Brown & Co Ltd, Nine Mile Point Colliery, Gwent. After nationalisation it worked at a number of South Wales sites and was scrapped at Hafodyrynys Colliery in May 1964.

Below. DOROTHY is spotted hiding in the bushes at Pontardawe Tinplate Works on Sunday 12 August 1962. It was built as a saddle tank by Brush Electrical Engineering, Loughborough, with the works number 301 in 1903 for Powlesland and Mason as their No.5 for use at Swansea Docks. It became GWR 795 at the grouping in 1923 and, in 1926, it was rebuilt as a pannier tank at Swindon Works. It was then sold on to W Gilbertson & Co Pontardawe Steel and Tinplate Works in 1929. Sadly this unusual locomotive was scrapped later in the year the photograph was taken.

Ex-GWR 2021 class 0-6-0PT 2092 stands out of steam at NCB Bargoed Colliery on Saturday 6 April 1963. Perhaps it never worked again as its smokebox door handles are missing. 2092 was one of a number of older second-hand pannier tank types that could still be found in South Wales. It had been built as a saddle tank at Wolverhampton Works in 1901 and after withdrawal by BR in August 1955 it was bought by the NCB early the following year for use at Bargoed. Apart from a very short stay at Groesfaen Colliery, it spent the rest of its working life there until it was finally scrapped in the second half of 1964.

2021 class 0-6-0PT 2034 sits inside the shed at NCB Blaenavon Colliery on Saturday 6 April 1963. Interestingly it still retains its smokebox and cabside number plates. It was built as a saddle tank at Wolverhampton Works in 1897 and withdrawn in September 1955. It was then bought by the NCB for use at the Caerphilly Tar Distribution Plant but was later transferred to Hafodyrynys Colliery and then to Blaenavon where it was scrapped in March 1964. There is some doubt whether the class, as saddle tanks, was designed by George Armstrong or William Dean.

Ex-Great Western Railway
9: Side Tanks

'Small Prairie' 4500 class 2-6-2T 4564 waits for action at Gloucester Central station on Saturday 4 January 1964, just three days after the first 'Top of the Pops' was broadcast on BBC TV. This type of tank engine was designed for the Great Western Railway by George Jackson Churchward and introduced in 1906. Seventy-five of these relatively light locomotives were built at Swindon and Wolverhampton works. They were intended mainly for use on branch line passenger trains.

4564 again four weeks later, on Saturday 1 February 1964, this time at Gloucester Horton Road shed (85B). Beside it is eight month old Cardiff Canton (86A) allocated Hymek diesel-hydraulic D7085 constructed by Beyer Peacock and behind is 5979 CRUCKTON HALL. 1444 can be seen on the left. 4564 was built in 1924 at the GWR Swindon Works and was the last of its class in BR service being withdrawn in September 1964.

Already preserved, 4555 arrives at Knowle & Dorridge station on a regular BR service train which terminated there on Monday 27 April 1964. This was the 17:28 from Birmingham Snow Hill which arrived at Knowle and Dorridge at 17:53. 4555 was built in 1924 and withdrawn in December 1963 when it was bought by Patrick Whitehouse and Pat Garland for preservation and based for a while at Tyseley shed (2A) where it was used on some local services. It was moved to Devon in October 1965 and hauled the Dart Valley Railway official opening train in 1969. It is now named WARRIOR and is based on the Dartmouth Steam Railway.

4569 has just arrived at Cardigan on the 15:40 all stations departure from Whitland on Saturday 11 August 1962. The train was timetabled to arrive at 17:16, a journey time of one hour thirty-six minutes even though it was only $27\frac{1}{2}$ miles away but there were nine intermediate stations or halts. 4569 was built at Swindon Works in 1924 and at this time was allocated to Neyland depot (87H). It was withdrawn from service in August 1964 and scrapped. Cardigan station was opened on 31 August 1886 as the terminus of the Whitland and Cardigan Railway. Passenger services ended just four weeks after this photograph was taken, on 10 September 1962, but goods traffic continued until the following May. The River Teifi can be seen in the background.

5563 is seen on Yeovil Town shed (72C) on Wednesday 8 April 1964. It was built at Swindon in 1928 as one of 100 4575 class locomotives which were a Collett development of the 4500 class and easily identifiable by the sloping top front of the side tanks. 5563 was withdrawn from Yeovil Town in December 1964. Yeovil Town station closed in October 1966 and the site of the station and shed is now occupied by a leisure centre and car park.

Collett 5101 class Prairie tank 4171 is in steam at its home depot, the four road Leamington Spa shed (84D), in the Summer of 1962. This was the year before the shed was transferred to the LM region and became 2L. 4171 was built at Swindon Works in 1949 and withdrawn in October 1964. The 1960 Derby built 08 diesel shunter, D3950, seen alongside later became 08782 and was named CASTLETON WORKS. It was offered for sale by DB Cargo in September 2016 and I believe it is now at Barrow Hill. The shed closed in June 1965.

Two years later, on Saturday 4 April 1964, Prairie tank 4171 makes a spirited start from Stratford-upon-Avon on the 08:43 local to Leamington Spa. It was a short turn for the driver and fireman taking just thirty-two minutes despite stopping at all five intermediate stations. Of particular interest is the leading coach, ex-LNER Diagram 115 Gresley designed third corridor (TK) coach E12659E, which ran on this service for a while. This wooden panelled vehicle was built in the early 1930s and had an external door for each of its eight compartments and four more on the, visible, corridor side.

5101 class Prairie tank 4120 from Tyseley (84E) shed has an easy task on a very light load leaving Stratford-upon-Avon towards Wilmcote on Friday 7 September 1962. It was built in 1937 and withdrawn in November 1964. Flower's brewery building is clearly seen on the skyline on the left. It had become part of the Whitbread empire in 1961 and brewing ended in January 1969. There was a serious fire the following July and the brewery was demolished a few years later. Behind the locomotive is the water tower and to the right one of the town's gas holders.

On Thursday 20 May 1965, Worcester (85A) allocated 4113 is in charge of a one coach local passenger train waiting to leave Moreton-in-Marsh. Nicknamed the 'Madman' by locals, the train had left Honeybourne at 17:50 and arrived at Moreton-in-Marsh at 18:12. Strangely, the run to Moreton, stopping at Chipping Campden and Blockley Halt, was in the Western Region timetable but the return to Honeybourne was empty stock. The station was opened by the Oxford, Worcester and Wolverhampton Railway (OWW) on 4 June 1853. 4113 was built at Swindon in 1928 and withdrawn in November 1965.

4113 had also been in charge of the 'Madman' the previous week, on Thursday 13 May 1965. It is seen here starting out from Moreton-in-Marsh on the returning non-timetabled empty stock to Honeybourne. The locomotive for this turn was usually the Honeybourne banker and could at times be a 22xx 0-6-0, a Hall or a Grange. The site of the Shipston-on-Stour branch, previously part of William James' horse-drawn Stratford and Moreton tramway which was officially opened on 5 September 1826, is on the left.

Collett 6100 class 2-6-2T 6111 has just passed the Clifford Sidings signal box near Stratford on the Stratford-upon-Avon and Midland Junction Railway line in charge of the Railway Enthusiasts' Club 'The Chiltern 200' excursion on Saturday 14 September 1963. The tour had started from Oxford Rewley Road station and it ran via Bicester, Chipping Norton, Kingham, Moreton-in-Marsh, Honeybourne, Stratford-upon-Avon (SMJR), Kineton, Fenny Compton, Banbury, Kings Sutton, Hook Norton and back, Banbury General, Brackley, Verney Junction, Grendon Underwood Junction, Princes Risborough and Chinnor and back, before returning via Thame to Oxford. 6111 was built in 1931 and was withdrawn in December 1965.

Large Prairie tank 6115 on a coal train passes the impressive Hafodyrynys Colliery buildings on the now closed Pontypool Road to Aberdare High Level line on Saturday 6 April 1963. The colliery closed in 1966 though the washery continued in use for a few more years. The site was finally cleared in 1985. The locomotive, shedded at Pontypool Road (86G), was built at Swindon in 1931 and was withdrawn in November 1964. This class of seventy locomotives was a development of the 5101 class with higher boiler pressure.

8109 waits at Birmingham Snow Hill station on a parcels train on Friday 14 August 1964 while the 09:22 passenger train bound for Wolverhampton departs from platform five. Snow Hill was the Great Western Railway station in Birmingham. Originally opened as Livery Street station in 1852, and renamed in 1858, it was rebuilt in 1871 and again between 1906 and 1912. It was closed in 1972 and demolished a few years later. In 1987 it was reopened for local trains totally rebuilt as a new station. 8109 was one of a class of ten Prairie tank locomotives introduced in 1938 which were rebuilt engines of a design by George Jackson Churchward dating back to 1903. 8109 was originally 3115 built in 1905 and later became 5115 before rebuilding in November 1939. It was withdrawn from service in June 1965.

5206 is ready to depart from Pontypool Road yard on Monday 12 April 1965. The 5205 class 2-8-0T specifically designed for hauling coal trains from the collieries in the South Wales valleys to the ports was a Collett development of the Churchward designed 4200 class. 5206 was built at Swindon in 1923 and withdrawn, from Pontypool Road shed (86G), the month after this photograph was taken. The imposing building is the County Hospital, Griffithstown, which was originally built as a workhouse.

5600 class 6643 crosses Walnut Tree Viaduct on the Swansea Railway Circle 'Rambling 56' rail tour on Saturday 31 July 1965. This tour had started at Cardiff General and ran to Senghenydd, Taff Merthyr, Dowlais, Bargoed, Nine Mile Point and ended at Newport High Street. The impressive viaduct with its seven steel lattice spans crossing the River Taff was built for the Barry Railway in 1901 to a design by Sir James Szlumper. It was closed in 1969 and dismantled over a few years. 6643 was built at Swindon in 1928 and was withdrawn in August 1965.

Clearly ex-works, 5600 class 5659 stands at Swindon on Sunday 7 April 1963 before returning to its home shed at that time, Pontypool Road (86G). It had been built at Swindon in 1926 and it was withdrawn in November 1965 and cut up by Cashmore's at Great Bridge. This class of two hundred 0-6-2 tank engines was designed by Charles Collett and they were built either at Swindon Works or for the GWR by Armstrong Whitworth. They were primarily intended for use in the South Wales valleys but they were to be found over much of the region.

0-4-2 tank locomotive 1440 is seen at Oswestry shed (89D) on Thursday 17 August 1961. It was built as one of a class of seventy-five Collett designed locomotives at Swindon and entered service in March 1935 as Great Western Railway 4840. It was withdrawn at the end of 1963 and scrapped.

1444 takes on water at Gloucester Horton Road shed (85B) on Saturday 1 February 1964. Several members of the class were allocated to this shed at the time to work the Gloucester Central to Chalford push-pull auto train service. 1444 was built at Swindon Works in 1935 as 4844. It was withdrawn in October 1964 and cut up around six months later. The 1960 Derby built 08 class diesel shunter behind, D3990, later became 08822.

1455 waits to depart from the ex-Great Western Gloucester Central station on the 11:20 all stations to Chalford on Saturday 15 February 1964. This Collett designed 0-4-2T was built at Swindon Works in 1935 as GWR 4855 and withdrawn in May 1964, just three months after I took this photograph. Gloucester Central was connected to the ex-Midland Railway Eastgate station by a long footbridge.

1453 has just passed Gloucester Horton Road shed (85B) and the Horton Road level crossing, also known as Tramway Crossing, on a Chalford local on Saturday 1 February 1964. Behind is the Horton Road gasworks gas holder and Tramway Junction signal box. 1453 was built at Swindon Works in 1935 as GWR 4853 and withdrawn in November 1964. The 1954 built auto trailer, W244W, was a Hawksworth designed A43 type. The signal box was to be replaced early in 1968 by the Gloucester Panel Box which was constructed opposite it.

1455 passes Gloucester Horton Road shed yard (85B) on a Chalford local just before the Horton Road level crossing on Saturday 1 February 1964. Gloucester Central station can be seen on the left with the spire of St Peter's Catholic church and the large station water tower rising above it. W223W, behind the locomotive, was a Hawksworth designed A38 auto coach.

1455 leaves Stonehouse Burdett Road station past the now closed Stonehouse Brick and Tile Company site on Saturday 15 February 1964 on the all stations 11:20 departure from Gloucester Central which was due to arrive at Chalford at 12:05. Note the Great Western centre-balanced semaphore signal. There was also a Stonehouse station on the ex-Midland Railway line, Oxford Road. The Hawksworth A38 auto coach W227W was built at Swindon in 1951.

1455 crosses paths with 1472 at the ex-GWR Stonehouse Burdett Road station on Saturday 15 February 1964. 1472 was pulling the 13:03 Gloucester Central departure which was due to arrive at Chalford at 13:45. 1455 was propelling the train which had left Chalford at 12:47 and was due to arrive at Gloucester Central at 13:32. 1472 was built at Swindon Works in 1936 as GWR 4872 and withdrawn in November 1964 after it was in charge of the very last train, the 23:20 Saturday only from Chalford on 31 October 1964 which arrived at Gloucester Central seventy minutes late.

Ex-Taff Vale Railway O1 class 0-6-2T 28 carries its National Coal Board identity 67 at Swindon Works on Sunday 20 September 1964. This Hurry Riches designed Taff Vale Railway locomotive was built at West Yard Works, Cardiff, in 1897 as TVR 28. It became GWR 450 when the TVR was absorbed into it at the 1923 grouping but it was sold for military use at the Woolmer Instructional Military Railway at Longmoor three years later and became WD205, and later WD70205, and named GORDON. At the end of the Second World War the engine was sold for service at South Hetton Colliery in County Durham. It was withdrawn as NCB 67 in 1960 and donated to BR for preservation. It is now part of the National Collection and has been based at several sites as TVR 28 once again.

Running on what was at the time still a British Railways line, Welshpool and Llanfair 2' 6" gauge 0-6-0 tank locomotive 1 THE EARL was built by Beyer Peacock Ltd of Gorton, Manchester, in 1902 with the works number 3496. It was renumbered as 822 by the Great Western Railway. The line was closed to traffic in November 1956 and its two locomotives were stored at Oswestry Works. 822 was not officially withdrawn by British Railways until August 1961. On 18 July 1961 it was returned to the line which the Welshpool and Llanfair Light Railway Preservation Company leased from BR from late 1962 until it was purchased in 1974. By the time this photograph was taken, at Castle Caereinion on Saturday 9 June 1962, the locomotive had regained its original number and it can still be seen, along with its sister 823, on the now preserved line which started operating on 6 April 1963.

Protected by a red flag, 1ft 11¾ in gauge Vale of Rheidol 2-6-2T 7 OWAIN GLYNDŴR crosses the road out of Aberystwyth station on the 10:00 to Devil's Bridge on Saturday 13 July 1963. The mainly uphill journey along the 1902 inaugurated 11¾ mile line took one hour. At this time the coaching stock was painted in Great Western 'chocolate and cream' livery. OWAIN GLYNDŴR was built, along with 8 PRINCE OF WALES, in 1923 at the Great Western Railway Swindon Works. They replaced two older locomotives on the line and, along with 9 LLEWELLYN, these were the last working steam engines in British Railways stock from the official end of main line steam in August 1968 until the Vale of Rheidol was privatised in 1989.